Let's I

In
to Sp

by

A. Ashiurakis

Darf Publishers Ltd
London
1984

First Edition 1966
Tenth Edition 1984

Printed and bound in Great Britain by
A. Wheaton & Co. Ltd., Exeter.

Preface

The lack of understanding each others language is considered the main barrier that prevents approach between people of different cast and thought. Therefore, the knowledge of a language undoubtedly leads to cordial relations between people who may come into contact with each other. This booklet is designed to meet the requirements of anyone wanting to acquire a working knowledge of everyday-spoken Arabic.

The pocket-book, in addition to being informative, also gives information of importance to potential visitors to Egypt – for instance the section containing handy phrases. It does not include elaborate grammatical terms, rather, only those essential in helping a student to learn Arabic step-by-step.

The course provides a general outline of colloquial Arabic sentences and phrases, all in the idiom currently used by Arabs.

The student who avails himself of this course will find that it provides him with anything relating to business and social life, etc.

Finally, it is hoped that it may help those eager to learn spoken Arabic. Fluency will depend on one's determination to master this book in order to put it into every-day use.

ASHIURAKIS

New Edition

This new expanded edition of Spoken Arabic is as the same as the first one, but with few additions and changes which were deemed necessary. e.g. New essential words and phrases have been introduced in order to increase the number of vocabularies and group of exercises are to be found at the end of every lessons.

The drills and exercises which are entirely based on the lessons contained herein, should be attempted after going many times over the lessons thoroughly.

However, since this course is purely in conversational form, all the words, phrases and sentences ought to be repeated vocally until they are well mastered.

Take every opportunity to speak your Arabic, because skill in its use depends on practising what you have learnt.

Ahmed Ashiurakis

Contents

CONTENTS

Abbreviations

ess.	lesson
m.	masculine
f.	feminine
s.	singular
pl.	plural
n.	noun
prep.	preposition
adj.	adjective
adv.	adverb
v.	verb
pa.	past
pre.	present
imp.	imperative
pp.	page
colloq.	colloquial

Note: The letters (m. and f.) indicate whether the word is masculine or feminine. This means that there are two genders. The feminine word generally ends in (a) as

Sadiqa = Friend
Moalima = Women-teacher

ALPHABET PRONOUNCIATION

English	Arabic	Name of letter
a		Alif
b		Bà
c		Tà
d		Thà
e		Jim
f		Hhà
g		Khà
h		Dàl
i		Thàl or dhal
j		Rà
k		Zà
l		Sin
m		Shin
n		Sad
o		Dàd
p		Ta
q		Tha
r		Ain
s		Ghain
t		Fà
u		Qaf ro Kàf
v		Kef
w		Lam
x		Mim
y		Nun
z		Hà
		Waw
		Ya

Guide to the Pronunciation of the Essential Arabic Alphabets

a	as in English ant	**f**	as in English fat
b	as in English bible	**g**	as in English quarrel
t – tha	as in English tab – thö	**k**	as in English king
thr	as in English threw	**l**	as in English life
j	as in English jail	**m**	as in English man
h	as in English hot	**n**	as in English naked
kha	as in German Nacht	**he**	as in English hit – hat
d	as in English dab	**waw**	as in English wabble
th	as in English there	**ye**	as in English yes – yard
r	as in English rat	**ee**	as in English feet
z	as in English zero	**oo**	as in English foot
s	as in English same – scope	**aa**	as in English far
		e	as in English leg
sh	as in English she – shine	**ai**	as in English late
ss	as in English sac	**oo**	as in English loot
tha	as in English that – thaw	**a**	as in English mother
ta	as in English taboò	**i**	as in English bite
tha	as in English thaw	**w**	as in English when
'ain	as in English ain't	**i**	as in English hit
ghain	as in English gain	**ow**	as in English owl

3

LESSON 1

Essential Greetings

Good morning	*Sabaah' al kheir* (m. and f.)
Good day	*Na'haarak sa'-eed* (m.)
Good day	*Na'haarak Mabrook* (m.)
Good evening	*M'sa al kheir* (m. and f.)
Good night (when leaving)	*Amsa ala kheir*
Good night (when replying)	*Waanta Min Ahlu*
Hellò! (welcome)	*Ah-lan wa sah'-lan* (m. and f.)
Hellò! (in reply)	*Ah-lan-wa-sah'-lan* (m. and f.)
How are you?	*Keif-al-haal* (m. and f.)
	Keif Haalak (m.)
	Keif Haalik f.)
Fine – Good – well	*Taib kwais* (m.)
	Taiba kwaisa (f.)
Thank God	*Al Hamdu–lillah*
Not bad	*Mush-battal*
Thank you	*Shukran* (m.)
Not at all	*Afwan*
You are welcome	*Ah'-lan-wa-sa'h'lan*
Will you please ...	*Min-fath-lak* (m.)
	Min-fath-lik (f.)
(in reply to thank you) (not at all)	*La-shuker-ala'-wajib*
Please ...	*T'fathal* (m.) *T'fathali* (f.)
Yes	*Aywa* (colloq.)

5

Yes	*Na-am* (classic)
Excuse me	*An-ith-nack* (m.)
Excuse me	*An-ith-nick* (f.)
Certainly ⎫ By all means ⎭	*T'fathal* (m.) *t'fathali* (f.)
Good bye	*Ma'-assalama*
Good bye	*Ma'-assalama* (in reply)
By God. It is true.	*Wallahee, saheeh.*
What?	*Ma'*
What!	*Matha*

NOTES

(1) The word *min-fath-lack* is used when requesting a service or a favour from a second person. (*ack* is for male and *ick* is for female).

(2) The word *an-ith-nack* or *an-ith-nick* means "with your permission" or "by your leave".

(3) The word *'tfathal* means "accept the services I am offering you" or it is used when some one would say "after you" or "have a seat" cigarette or drink etc. and also "help yourself".

(4) The word *fee-aman-illah* means go under the protection of God and it is used in reply to *ma'-assalama* Good bye.

(5) The word (*hal*) is an interrogative particle.

(6) In asking a question, the word (*ma'*) – classic, is sometimes more preferable than the word (*shinu*) the colloquial e.g.

what is your name? = *ma-asmak?*

LESSON 2

Vocabulary

Good, alright, well	*Kwais* (m.) *Kwaisa* (f.)
Morning	*Sabaah*
Day (referring to light)	*Nahaar* (s.)
Evening	*Lail* (s.) *Layaly* (pl.)
Night	*Masaa* or *Lail*
Dawn	*Fa'jer*
Today (the day)	*Alyom*
Tonight	*Al-leila* or *allaila*
Wealth or better (comparative)	*Kheir – Kheir min*
In front of you	*Ama mak* (m.)
And	*U* or *Wa*
How as like (prep.)	*Kaif*
Duty – duties	*Wajib – Wajibaat* (pl.)
what is ...?	*Ma'*
where is ...?	*Fain – Wein* or *Wain*
when ...?	*Amta'* or *Mata*
where ...?	*Wein*
which ...? what ...?	*Ain* or *Wein*
From where ...?	*Minain – Minfain*
To where ...	*Ila-fain*
who ...? whom ...?	*Mann*
when ... (adv.)	*Kaif* or *Lam-ma*
This is better than ...	*Hatha khair min ...*

Demonstratives & Pronouns

Unless	*Ma'-lam*
Whose ...?	*Li-mann* or *Mta'-mann*
This is ...	*Hathe* (m.) *Hathi* (f.)
That is ...	*Thaka* (m.) *Telka* (f.)
These are ...	*Hathihi*
Those are ...	*Hawlay* (m.)

I	*Ana*	My	*i* (suffixes)
You (m.s.)	*Anta*	Your	*ak* (m.)
He	*Huwa*	His	*ah*
She	*Heya*	Her	*ha*
We	*Na'hna* or *Na'hnu*	Our	*na*
You (f.s.)	*Anti*	Your	*ik* (f.)
You (f.pl.)	*Anten*	Your	*kun* (f.)
You (m.pl.)	*Antum*	Your	*kum* (m.)
They (m.)	*Hum*	Their	*hoom* (m.)
They (f.)	*Henn*	Their	*henn* (f.)

N.B.

There is no Arabic word for the indefinite (a or an); e.g.

a pencil = *Kalam*	an egg = *baida*
a book = *kitaab*	an inkpot = *mahbara*

(It is) is either masculine *huwa or*
                feminine *heya*

LESSON 4

Possessive Pronouns

The word *mta'* which means "belong" or "property of" can be used as a possessive pronoun by suffixing those suffixes shown on lesson 3 e.g.

Whose book is this?	*Bita men hathal kitaab?*
It is mine	*Bitai*
Mine	*Bitai* or *Lee* or (*Leeya*)
Yours (m.)	*Bitaak* or *Lack*
Yours (f.)	*Bitaak* or *lik*
Yours (m.pl.)	*Bitakum* or *Elkum*
Yours (f.pl.)	*Bitakin* or *Elken*
His (the "h" is aspirated)	*Bitahu* or *La'h*
Hers (accent on the (a))	*Bitaha* or *La'ha*
Ours	*Bitana* or *La'na*
Theirs (m.)	*Bitahum* or *La'hum*
Theirs (f.)	*Bitahur Mta-hen* or *La'hen*

N.B.

Do not use the verb "to be" in the present tense i.e. (it is) is omitted (see lesson 3).

There is another possessive pronoun viz. the letter (L) by suffixing the endings shown on lesson 3 e.g. mine = *lee* or *li* – which means "for me" "yours" *lak*. They also mean *to me, To you etc.; e.g.*

My book	*Kitaabi* or *Kitaabee*
My chair	*Kursi-i* or *Kursee*
My pencil	*Ghalami* or *Ghalamee*

The Verb To Have

The word "and" which means "at" or "with" or in the "possession of" can be used with noun suffixes shown in lesson 3 to denote "the verb to have" e.g.

I have a book   Andi Kitaab

There is no need to use the Nominative Pronouns with the verb "To have" in Arabic.

To make the Past Tense of the verb "to have" i.e. I had. You had etc., just add, the word *"kana"* or *kan* as a prefix to the word *and;* e.g.

I had a pencil   *Kan andi Kalam*

You had a book   Kan andak kitaab

But for the Future Tense the prefix *"ikoon"* is used. e.g. I shall have a pencil. *ikoon andi Kalam* or the word (*sa*) is used as a prefix to *"ikoon"*.

I shall have a pencil tomorrow. *sa'ikoon andi Kalam ghadan*.

All the same	*Ala haddin sawaa*
Till now – up to now	*Lihad al aan*
You are wrong	*Al hak alaik*
How do you call this?	*Aish asm hatha*
What is the name of this?	*Ma asm hatha*
I hope (it is) true	*Na'-mal yakoon saheeh*
Give me a receipt	*Atini wasl*

LESSON 5

Numbers

0	*Sifr*	11	*Eh-Dash*
1	*Wahad*	12	*At-nash*
2	*Et-nein*	13	*T'lataash*
3	*T'laata*	14	*Arba-tash*
4	*Arba'-a*	15	*Khams-tash*
5	*Khamsa*	16	*Sitta-sh*
6	*Sitta'*	17	*Saba-tash*
7	*Sab'-a*	18	*T'man-tash*
8	*T'manya*	19	*T'ssa-tash*
9	*T'ssa'-a*	20	*Ash-reen*
			or *Ish-reen*
10	*Ash-ra*	21	*Wahad wa ashreen*

NEGATIVE PARTICLE: (*MUSH*)

The word *mush* meaning "not" is used to negate a phrase or a sentence. It is a prefix and is also used before adjectives e.g.

He is not going to ...	*Huwa mush Raih ila ...*
I am not coming to ...	*Ana mush jei ila ...*
It is not good – nice	*Mush Kuweis*
It is not that etc.	*Da Mush Hua*
School (s.)	{ *Madrasa* (s.)
	Madaars (pl.)
Office (s.)	*Maktib* (s.) *Makaatib* (pl.)

LESSON 6

Verb To Be

NEGATIVE FORM

I am not a doctor	*Lastoo tabeeb*
You are not ... (m.s.)	*Anta Mush* (add any noun)
He is not ...	*Mush* or *Mahoosh*
She is not a doctor	*Mush tabeeba*
We are not soldiers	*Mish asaaker*
You are not (m.pl.)	*Antum lastoom*
You are not (f.pl.)	*Antunna lastoonna*
You are not (f.s.)	*Anti lasti*
They are not (m.)	*Laisa hoom*
They are not (f.)	*Laisa hoonna*

VOCABULARY

Thirsty	*Atshaan*	Easy	*Saa-hell*
Hungry	*Ja-an*	Difficult	*Sa'-ab*
Lazy	*Kaslaan*	Busy	*Mashghoul*
Bad	*Radee*	Business	*Shughl*
Good	*Jaid (Kuais)*	Task	*Shughl*
Satiate	*Shab-ann*	Work	*Amel*
Angry	*Za'-lan*	Rich	*Ghane'e*
Tired	*Ta'-baan*	Poor	*Faqeer*
True	*Sa'-heeh*	Correct	*Sa'-heeh*
A piece of			
iron	*Hadeed*	Story	*Hekaaya*
Incident	*Haditha*	Heavy	*Thaqeel*

12

Light			
(weight)	*Khafeef*	Grass	*Ashab*
Student	*Tilmeeth*	Opium	*Afiuun*

Exercises Based on Lessons 1 to 6

(1) Translate the following words into Arabic:

Good morning. Hello! How are you? Not bad. Thank you. To day. To night. Where are you? From where are you (m.)? Count the cardinal numbers from 1 to 20. What is your name? I am not going to school.

(2) Change orally the following Arabic words into feminine:

Atshaan   Ta-baan   Thaqeel   Khafeef   Wahid Ghanee   Faqeer   Shab'-an   Za'-lan   Sadeeq Sa-heeh   Radee   Sa-ab   Tabeeb   Tilmeeth

(3) Answer in Arabic the following questions:

Limann hathal-kitaab?   Hall hatha-kitaabak? Hal-anta-at-shan? Ma'-asmak?   Keif-halak? Hal-andik-kitaab?   An-ith-nick.   Ma-assalama! Hal-hatha qalamik?

(4) Memorise the following:

The separate personal pronouns: *ana, anta,* etc. The possessive pronouns shown in lesson 3 with a noun, e.g. *kitaab* = a book, *kitaabi, kitaabak* = my book, your book, etc.
The verb to have (*and*) with the suffixes i, ak, ah, etc., and then the Past Tense of the Verb to have with the same suffixes i.e. *kan andi* = I had etc.

LESSON 7

Comments on Lesson 4

Nouns and adjectives can be made feminine by suffixing the letter (a) for the singular and (at) for the plural ... e.g.

I am thirsty	*Ana atshan* (m.)
I am thirsty	*Ana atshana* (f.)
I am not thirsty	*Ana Gheir atshan* (m.)
I am not thirsty	*Ana Gheir atshana* (f.)

Interrogatives are generally made by tone of voice or the prefix *"Hal"* but this is rather classic e.g.

Are you thirsty ...?	*Hal anta atshan ...?*
Yes, I am thirsty	*Aywa atshan*
No, I am not thirsty	*La' Gheir atshan*
Is the lesson easy?	*Addaars saa-hell ...?*
No, it is difficult	*La' sa'-ab*

Sometimes (it is) is omitted see lesson 4.

Which of us	*Ay-minna*
Which of you (m.pl.)	*Ay-minkum*
Which of them (m.)	*Ay-minhum*
Chief of the tribe	*Sheik-kabila*
Desert	*Sah'-ra* (s.) *Sahaari* (pl.)
Tent (s.)	*Khey-ma* (s.) *Khiyaam* (pl.)
Word	*Kalima* (s.) *Kalimaat* (pl.)
I am alone	*Li-wah-di*

VOCABULARY

Other(s)	*Akher* (s.) *Akhereen* (pl.)
Another	*Wahad-akher* (m.)
	Wahada-akhrà (f.)
Where is the other man?	*Fein arajel lakher*
Please, call another man	*Minfath-lak naadi*
	Rajel wahad-akher
Call the others	*Naadi al-akhereen*
Take your time (m.)	*Ala-mah-lak* (m.s.)
Take your time (f.)	*Ala-mah-lik* (f.s.)
Whatever the case may be	*Mah-ma kana alamr*
I (shall) see you some day	*Enshoofak fi yom min alayam*
From day to day	*Min yom liyom*
Away with you please	*Ibta-id anni minfath-lak*
I am at your disposal	*Ana tihet-amrak* (m.)
First class man	*Rajel mum-taaz*
It is high time for us to go now	*Aana-la'-wan li-nath-hab Halan*
Sometimes	*Ba-ath-al-waght* (or)
	Ah-yaanan
I am busy (sometimes)	*Ah-yaanan ana-mash-ghool*
Anyhow come	*Ala-kulli-haal ta-aal*
Later on	*Ba-dien*
Impossible	*Ghair-mum-ken* (or)
	Musta-heel
I cannot help it	*Ma-biddi-heela*
It cannot be helped	*Ma-bil-yad-heela*
Have you any proof?	*Andak-bur-haan?*
Indeed, I have	*Fi-alan-andi* (or) *Ay-wa*
Unknown	*Maj-hool* (m.)
At last,	*Wa-akheeran*
You are right	*Al-hack-ma-ack*
Might is right	*Al-hack-ma-alquwa'*
My friend	*Ya-sadeeki*

15

Vocabulary

	S	P
Pen(s)	*Ghalam*	*Aghlaam*
Box(s)	*Sandook*	*Sanadeek*
Key(s)	*Meftaah*	*Mafateeh*
Book(s)	*Kitaab*	*Koutub*
Pencil	*Kalam*	*Aklam*
Chair(s)	*Koursi*	*Karaasi*
Table(s)	*Towla*	*Towlaat*
Bed(s)	*Fraash*	*Frashaat*
Door(s)	*Ba'-ab*	*Beebaan — abwaab*
Window(s)	*Shubbak*	*Shababek*
Window(s)	*Naafitha*	*Nuwaafith*
Week(s)	*Isboo*	*Asabee*

NOTES

There are four letters which denote the definite article: viz. (l, al, el, il) all mean (the).

These letters are "prefixs" to nouns and they become evident before any word beginning with these letters: (a, j, kh, gh, b, h, f, q, m, n, w, k, y). They are called lunar letters.

Lunar Vocabulary

The lion	*Al asad*	The rat	*Al faar*
The camel	*Al jamal*	The moon	*Al ghamar or qamar*

LESSON 9

Vocabulary

The lamb	*Al kharoof*	The key	*Al muftah*
The crow	*Al ghuraab*	The chair	*Al kursee*
The mule	*Al baghl*	The rose	*Al warda*
The horse	*Al hessan*	The pyramid	*Al ah-raam*
The sparrow	*Al asfoor*	The hand	*Al yed*

But note the definite article assimilates before these letters which are called (sun letters) i.e. solar letters. (t, d, th, z, s, sh, r, l, n) i.e. the sound is doubled.

Solar Vocabulary

The crown	*At-taaj*	The noon	*Ath-thohr*
The bear	*Ad-dubb*	The rice	*Ar-rozz*
The cobra	*At-a'ban*	The morning	*Assabaah*
The wolf	*Ath-theeb*	The limon	*Al-limoon*
The oil	*Az-zeit*	The plane	*At-tayara*
The sun	*Ash-shams*	The fire	*An-naar*
The sugar	*Assucr*		

N.B.

Generally a feminine word in the singular ends either in "h" aspirated or in "a" accented e.g.

A table	*Towla* or *towla'*	A school	*Madrsa'*
A map	*Kharita'*	A newspaper	*Jarida'*
A picture	*Soora*	A room	*Ghourfa'*
A station	*Ma-hatta'*		or *Hujra'*

LESSON 10

The Genitive Case

When a noun is used to form the genitive case, the "h" or the "a" becomes "t" e.g.

Ali's table	*Tawlat Ali*
The camel of Ali	*Ja'mal Ali*

The word (*Ja'mal*) is masculine.

The preposition (of) is *mta'*. It can be used instead of the above examples e.g.

The pen of Ali	*Ghalam Bita Ali*
The book of Ali	*Kitaab Bita Ali*
The office of Ali	*Makteb Bita Ali*

N.B.

The Arabs have the duality which does not exist in any other language. So in order to express two nouns or two things use the word «EIN or AIN» it is suffixed to the singular noun in the accusative and genitive case.

Two keys	*Muftahein* (m.)	Two roses	*Wa'rdatein* (f.)
Two books	*K'taabein* or	Two sparrows	*Asfoorein* (m.)
	Kitaabein (m.)	Two pens	*Ghalamein* (m.
Two tables	*Towltain* (f.)	Two words	*Kalimatein* (f.)

e.g. Please give me two keys
Minfath-lak atini muftahein

I have two tables	*Andi towltein*
I have two chairs	*Andi koursi-ein*
He has two lambs	*Anda kharoofein*

18

LESSON 11

The Days of the Week

Monday	*Yom-al-et'nein*
Tuesday	*Yom-al-talaat*
Wednesday	*Yom-al-erbaha*
Thursday	*Yom-al-khamees*
Friday	*Yom-al-jum-aa*
Saturday	*Yom-al-sabt*
Sunday	*Yom-al-a'had*
Today (This day)	*Alyom*
Tomorrow	*Bukra – Ghadan*
Yesterday	*Ams*
The day before yesterday	*Awelams*
After tomorrow	*Ba'-ad Bukra*
Noon	*Theher* (or) *Thaha'r*
Mid-day	*Ness-Nahaar* (or) *Nessif nahaar*
Afternoon	*Ba'-d ath-theher* (or) *Adduher*
Beforenoon	*Ghabel ath-theher*
Every day	*Kulyom*
Every other day	*Yom ba'-d yom*
Every week(s)	*Kull-asboo' – asaabea* (pl.)
Every month(s)	*Kull-sha'-har – shihoor* (pl.)
Every year(s)	*Kull-sa'na – sineen* (pl.)

LESSON 12

Kinship

Vocabulary

Man – Men	*Rajel – Reejaal*
Woman – Women	*Sit – Sittaat*
Boy – Boys	*Walad – Awlaad*
Girl – Girls	*Bint – Banaat*
Son – Sons	*Ibn – Abna'a*
Daughter – Daughters	*Ibna' – Banaat*
Child – Children	*T'full – At'faal*
Brother – Brothers	*Akh – Ikhwan*
	(or) *Ikhwa*
Sister – Sisters	*Ukht – Khawaat*
Father – Fathers	*Ab – Abaa*
Mother – Mothers	*Um – Um-mahaat*
Friend – Friends (m.)	*Sadeeq – Asdeqaa*
Friend – Friends (f.)	*Sadeeqa – Sadiqaat*
How many	*Kam* (for number)
How much	*Kam* (for quantity)

N.B.

The word *beish* or *kam* may be used for price. *kam* takes the singular. e.g. How many books have you? *kam kitaab andak?*

LESSON 13

Conservation

RENTING A HOUSE

I have a friend	*Andi sadeeq*
He is an American	Hoowa Amreekani
He asked me	*Sa'-alani*
To find him a nice house	*nalghala beit kuweis*
Where (does) he want it?	*Wein ireeda . . .?*
Near the Embassy	*Ghareeb as-safara*
If it is possible . . .	*Enkaan mumken*
When (do) you want it?	*Amta' t'reeda . . .?*
As soon as possible . . .	*Halan* (or) *bisur-á*
For (he is) coming	*Alashan (huwa) ja-ee*
After two days	*Ba-ad yomein*
Then, let me	*khallini*
see you	*enshoofak*
One day previous to that.	*Be voum ghabl*
O.K. alright.	*Taib ensha'lla*
Goodbye	*Ma'assalama*
Good-bye (reply).	*Fee amn Illah*

N.B.

The word (*beish*) is used here with the meaning of: (in order to) and the word (*ensha'lla*) means: If God will or I hope.

EXERCISES BASED ON LESSONS 7 to 13

(1) Translate verbally the following:

I am a doctor (m). He is not thirsty. This lesson is easy. (Which) of you is the chief of the tribe? This incident is not good. What is today? It is Friday. Give me a pencil, please. How many days are in the week? Where is my bed? This is my office and where is your office?

(2) Make the following Arabic nouns plural:

*(Ghalam)   Sandook   Koursee   Ba-ab
Tawla   Yom   Bint   Rajel   Sadeeq   Walad
Ukht   Moos   Zeit*

(3) Write down the days of the week in Roman script and then compare them with lesson 11:

(4) Answer in Arabic the following questions:

*Kam walad andak?   Fein sadiqak al-yom?
                Hal-hatha-arrajel kwais?   Amta-
jei-ila-al-maktib?   Why?   Hal-anta-mash-ghool?
Hal-huwa-rajel-mum-taaz?   Wein-al-awlaad-mta-
ak?   Hal-al-madrasa-nathifa?*

(5) Add the definite article to the following words and then compare them with the lunar or the solar lessons:

*Taaj   Shams   Succr   Naar   Warda   Asfoor
Muftah   Kharoof   Jamel   Faar   Qamar
Theeb   Sabaah   Bab   Tawla   Koursee
Mahatta*

22

LESSON 14

Office Conservation

Good morning	*Sabaah al kheir*
I wish to see the director,	*Ureed enshoof al mudeer*
or the secretary of the	*Ow as-segretair* (m.)
company.	
Sorry!	*Aasef*
The director	*Sayed al mudeer*
is not in	*mush moujood*
When do you think	*Amta' tefteker*
he will come . . .?	*ejee*
I am afraid I do not know	*Aasef ma'narefsh*
Please have a seat.	*T'fathal ejles*
What can I do for you.	*Ay-khedma?*
Thank you.	*Shukran*
I shall come later – then.	*Enjee ba'dein*
O.K. alright	*Tayib*
Good bye	*Ma'assalama*
Goodbye (reply).	*Ma'assalama*

N.B.

The word (*sayed*) means Mr.

The phrase (*ay-khedma*) literally means:
(*any service*).

LESSON 15

NOTES ON LESSONS 13 and 14

(1) The word (*enkaan*) *mumken*: means literally "were it possible". It indicates an improbable condition.

   enkaan means "if" and *mumken* "may be".

(2) The word *kull* meaning "all or every or each" can take pronoun suffixes (see lesson 3) e.g.

   All of them,   all of you   *kullhum*   *Kull'kum*

(3) *Taib* is a common form of "yes" meaning "alright" or "Good".

(4) *Urid* or *enreed* means I want. I wish.

(5) Auxiliaries like, shall, will, do, does etc. particularly in the negative form, are generally omitted.

(6) When demonstratives are used as in:

   This book   *Hathal kitaab*   This boy *Hathal alwalad* etc. the noun takes the definite article in Arabic, thus:

   This the book – This the boy – This the pencil.

(7) The word *'ensha'-alla* is used for future events. e.g. I hope I shall see you. *Enshalla – enshoofak.*
   Tomorrow   *Burka*   I hope too   *Ensha'alla*

(8) *Months:*

December	*Dicember*	June	*Younyou*
January	*Yannair*	July	*Youlyou*
February	*Febrire*	August	*Augustus*
March	*Maar's*	September	*September*
April	*Abreed*	October	*October*
May	*Mayou*	November	*Noovember*

LESSON 16

Time

What is the time, please.	*Sa'-a kam min fathlak*
(It is) two o'clock	*Sa'-a et-nein*
Then what time can I see you	*Izan sa'-a kam aghdar enshoofak*
Come at quarter to three at my office	*Ta'-aalatalata illa rooba' tee maktabi*
Sorry, I cannot because	*Asef La Aqdir alashan*
I have no watch.	*Ma'andish sa'-a*
Take mine and come at half past three.	*Khuth mtai wa ta'aal sa'-a talata wa nus*

N.B.

The word *wa* or *u* is used for "past the hour" and *illa* for "to the hour".

ORDINAL NUMBERS

1st	*Awal*	6th	*Saades*
2nd	*Thani*	7th	*Saaba'*
3rd	*Thaaleth*	8th	*Thaamen*
4th	*Raaba'*	9th	*Taa'-sa*
5th	*Khaams*	10th	*Aasher*

The word *al* definite article (the) can be used to mean (the first etc.) e.g. *alawal. attain*

Here	*Hana'*	There	*Hanaak*

25

LESSON 17

More Greetings

(1) When admiration is to be expressed: such as "what a nice boy, girl, beautiful house – a nice car – etc. simply say: *masha-allah*, meaning, "By God's will".

(2) To greet someone who has just arrived or returned from a trip – hospital or safe from an accident say:

El'hamdu lillah bissalama the answer is: *Allah-essal-mak* (m.), meaning "welcome back".

(3) Congratulations   *Mabrook*
Thank you (reply)   *Allah ebaarik feek*
Happy new year   *Kul-sana' wanta taib*
To your health   *Fee sah'-tak* (m.)
Thank you reply)   *Allah' esalmak* or *Shukran*

(4) When passing by people or a place where people have come before you and to avoid shaking hands simply say. *Salam alaikum* which means, "peace be upon you". The answer to this salutation is *wa alaikum assalam*. However this greeting is used for men only.

(5) Do you speak English?   *Hal tatakalm Ingleezi?*
I speak a little   *Natakalam shewaya*
I understand a little   *Naf-ham shewaya*
May I use the   *Mumken nasta-mel*
    telephone?   *attalafoon?*
What do you say?   *Aysg t'ghool?*
Nothing   *La-shay!*
Your name please?   *Asm al kareem?*

N.B.

It is a polite form to ask one's name by saying (*asm al kareem*) or (*asm hath-ratak*). (*hath-ratak*) means Your-goodself. *Hath-ratakum* means your goodselves.

(6) I introduce Mr. . . . *En-arfak be assayed . . .*
    we are honoured
        (reply) *Tscharafna*
    Honour *Sharaf*

The word *tcharafna sharaf* "we are honoured" is the reply to that introductive or it can be simply *ahlan wa sa'hlan* meaning "welcome" which literally means *ahl* = Family and *'sa'hlan* = easily.

(7) Pardon me *Samih'-ni* (m.) *Sam'hini* (f.)
    Excuse me *Samih'-ni* (m.) *Sam'hini* (f.)
    I regret *Muta'-asef* (m.)
    I regret *Muta'asefa* (f.)
    Pardon me! *Afwan*
    I beg your pardon *Afwan*
    Dear (beloved) *Azizi* (m.) *Azizi* (f.)

(8) In order to express an exclamation such as:
    what a fine day! *Ya-salam! nahaar jameel*
    to day *Alyom*
    what a beautiful sight! *Ya-salam! manthar jameel*

(9) I am ready. *ana hathar*
    hathar, means (I am present)
    However, when *hathar* is used alone, it is a respected
    way of assenting to an order or a request e.g. I want
    to come early. *Enreedak t'jee bakree.*

    alright O.K. *Hathar.*

(10) The word *ya* means "O!" is used to call some one's attention. e.g. *ya* Ahmed = O! Ahmed.

What a pity!	*Ya-lil-asef!*
What a nice book this is	*Jameel hathal kitaab!*

(11) Who are you? *Hath-ratak men?* (or) *Men hathratak* (m.). This is a form of courteous address.

(12) Numbers.

22	*Et nein wa ish reen*		
29	*Tes-a wa ishreen*		
30	*Talateen*		
39	*Tes-a wa talateen*		
40	*Arbaeen*		
50	*Khamseen*		
60	*Siteen*		
70	*Sab-een*		
80	*Tamaneen*		
90	*Tes-een*		
100	*Mia'*	101	*Mia wa wahed*
200	*Mitein*	110	*Mia wa ashra*
300	*Talatmia*	129	*Mia wa tesa*
400	*Arbamia*		*Wa ish-reen*
1.000	*Alf*		
2.000	*Alfein*		
1.000.000	*Melyoun*	2.000.000	*Melyounein*

What place is this?	*Ma hathal makaan?*
Where is the town?	*Fein al madeena?*
Go straight on?	*Emshi ala Tul*
Go back or	*Emshi law-ra* (or)
Turn back	*Argia*
Postage(s)	*Taa-ba' – tawa-ba* (pl.)
Please give me	*Atini min fath-lak*
that letter	*Hathak ajawaab*
Letter	*Risaala*

LESSON 18

Conversation

POLICE STATION

Station(s)	*Markez* (s.) *Maraakez* (pl.)
Police(man)	*Boolees* or *Shoorti*
Where is the Police Station?	*Fein markez al boolees?*
	Fein markez al ahsoorta
Nothing wrong!	*Laa-baas*
I have lost my wallet	*Dhaiatu Mihfazati*
When . . . ?	*Mata*
Now!	*Al-aan*
Come with me quickly	*Ta'-al maee Bisur-a*
In order to show you	*Hatta wareek*
Where I lost it?	*Ain Dhaiatana?*
Oh, thank you	*Shurkran*
Not at all	*Al-afoo* (or) *Afwan*
Tell me is it far away?	*Gully huwa baeed?*
No, very near	*La', ghareeb jiddan*
(Shall) I take my car?	*Nakhooth sayar-ti?*
There is no need	*Mafish luzoom*
because the station (is)	*Li-anna al markez*
in the same street.	*Fi nafs ashaara*
We must not waste time	*Mush laazim Nudaia waghut*
In case it is picked up.	*Yomken yakhuduhu ahad*
You are right	*Andak hagh*
Let us go immediately.	*Ithan haya bina namshio bisur-a*

LESSON 19

NOTES

(1) The word *(jiddan)* meaning (very) may be used with adjectives, e.g.

Very big man	*Rajel Kebeer jiddan*
It is very cheap.	*Rakhees jiddan*
Very expensive	*Ghaali jiddan*

N.B.

The adjectives are used after nouns.

(2) The word "still" *mazaal* is used with verbs

I (am) still reading my book	*Mazaal Akkra fi kitaabi*
I (have) not yet found my place	*Mazelt ma wajadtsh* (1) *makaani*

(1) see lesson 5 Negative particles.

(3) Verb To Be.

I was	*Ana kunt*	You were	*Anta kunt* (m.s.)
He was	*Huwa kaan*	She was	*Hya kaanat*
We were	*Nahna kunna*	You were	*Antu kuntu* (m.p)
You were (f.)	*Anten kunten*	You were	*Anti kunti (f.s.)*
They were (m.)	*Hum kaanu*	They were	*Hen kaanan* (f.p

(4) The following two particles are used to negate verbs in the present and past tenses:

(*ma————sh.*) These are equivalent to: don't, didn't, has not, shall not, will not etc.

Any verb used must be placed between those two
particles, e.g.

I cannot go there.	*Ana managhdarsh Aemshi hanaak.*
I do not write Arabic.	*Ana maaktibsh arabi.*
I was not here.	*Ana ma kuntsh hana*
We were not there there	*Nahna ma kunnash hanaak Hanaak.*
Were you not there?	*Makuntsh anta hanaak?*
I have not a pen.	*Ma endish ghalam.*
I found my book.	*Wajat kitaabi*
I did not find my book there.	*Ma wajatsh kitaabi hanaak*
I went there.	*Masheit hanaak.*
I did not go there.	*Lam Azhab hanaak*
She had a box	*Hya kaan endaha sandoogh*
She had not a box	*Ma kaanish endaha sandoogh*
A note-book	*Daf-tr* (s.) *Dafaatr* (pl.)
They speak English (m.)	*Hum yatakallamu inglizi*
They don't speak Arabic (m.)	*Hum mayatakallamush Arabi*
Officer(s)	*Thabit* (s.) *Thubaat* (pl.)

EXERCISES BASED ON LESSONS 14 to 19

(1) Translate verbally the following, phrases and sentences into Arabic:

My friend is (an) American. This (is) my embassy. One day before. I am afraid. I (do) not know. (A) girl. (A) boy. (A) day. (A) week. (A) month. My brother. I wish to see the director. Thank you. The time. Congratulation, O my dear friend! Excuse me.

(2) Memorise the cardinal numbers from 20 to 100.

(3) Answer the following questions in Arabic:

Hal andak sa'-a? Kam asa'-a al-aan? el-hamdu-lillah-bissalama, fein kunt ams? Hal anta hathar? Fein al medina, minfathlak? (Is) this your office?

(4) Put the following into negative:

Wajat kitaabi   Ana kunt hanaak   Dhaiatu Samih-ni   Ureed   Huwa thaabit Atakalam arabi   Andi qalam   Nek-tib arabi

(5) Transliterate the following verb:
I was. He was. You were. We were. She was. They were. I had. He had. You had. We had. She had. They had.

LESSON 20

Rules on Nouns and Adjectives

Most masculine regular nouns and adjectives form their feminine by suffixing the letter (a) singular and (at) plural e.g.

poor	*fakeer* or *faqeer*	poor	*fakeera* etc.
great	*atheem*	short	*kaseer*
clean	*natheef*	strong	*qawi* or *ghawi*
dirty	*wesikh*	weak	*tha'-eef*
long	*taweel*	small	*sagheer*
old (age)	*kabeer*	young	*sagheer*
old (things)	*qadeem*	rich	*ghanee*
new	*jadeed*	some	*baath* or *baad*
any	*aiee* or *ai*	someone	*waahad*
anyone	*aiwaahad*		

I have an old table.	*Andi tawala kadeema*
I want a new one.	*Urid wahda jadeeda*
This (is) an old man.	*Hatha rajal kabeer.*
Where (is) his young son?	*Wein ibnah as-sagheer?*
Have you a new chair?	*Andak kursi jadeed?*
Yes, I have.	*Aywa, andi*
That (is) a strong horse.	*Hathak hesan qawi*
The woman (is) rich.	*Asitt ghaneea or ghanya*
I have a nice suitcase	*Andi shanta kuweisa*

N.B. The word (at) is also suffixed to the foreign nouns for plural purpose e.g.

Bus	*Baas* (s.) *Baasaat* (pl.)
Telephone	*Telafoon* (s.) *Telafoonaat* (pl.)
Cinema	*Sinima* (s.) *Sinimaat* (pl.)
Television	*Televizion* (s.) *Televizionaat* (pl.)
Table	*Tawla* (s.) *Tawlaat* (pl.)

33

LESSON 21

Vocabulary

Private	*Khaas* (or) *Khusoosi*
Organisation	*Mou-a-sasa*
Company or Firm	*Sharika*
Market(s)	*Soog* (s.) *Aswaaq* (pl.)
Oil(s)	*Zeit* (s.) *Ziyout* (pl.)
Petrol	*Benzeen*
Field(s)	*Hackel – Huqool* (pl.)
Nation	*Watan – Awtaan* (pl.)
Prime Minister	*Raees al wazara*
Minister	*Wazir*
Under Secretary of State	*Wakil wazara*
Employee	*Muwathaf*
Government	*Hukuma*
Newspaper	*Jareeda*
News	*Akh-baar*
Magazine	*Majalla*
Ambulance	*Arabat Lissaff*
Advice	*Naseeha*
Court	*Mah'-kama*
Lawyer	*Muhamee*
Out of bounds	*Mam-noo'a*
Boundaries	*Hudood*
What do you say?	*Maza Taguool?*
What do you mean?	*Maza ta'-nee?*
What is that called?	*Maza asm hathak?*
What in English?	*Maza bil Engleezi?*
What in Arabic?	*Maza bil Arabi?*
What in Italian?	*Maza bil Itaali?*

LESSON 22

Prepositions and Their Use

Than, of, from since	Min
This book is better than that.	Hathal kitaab ah-san min hathak
I want to go from here.	Uridu Azhab min ha-na'
To, Towards	Ila
We went to the market	Masheina ila as-soogh
For, belonging to.	Li – Lil – L.
He died of (the) fever.	Maat min al humma
This place (is) for sleeping.	Hathal makaan lil nome
By	Bi – bil
Send this by post.	Ersel hatha bil bareed
With – On – Upon	Ma'a ala'
I was with him.	Kunt ma'a huwa
The food is on the table.	Atta'-am ala at-tawla
Between, among.	Bein (or) Ma'-bein
Between you and me.	Beini ou beinak
He (is) among the trees	Huwa ma bein lash-jaar
Under – below	Tehet (or) Tahet
The dog (is) under the chair	Al kalb tahet al kursi

LESSON 23

Prepositions

Over – Above	*Foguh* (or) *fough*
The lamp (is) over my head.	*Al-lamba fough raasi*
Before (time)	*Gable*
I came before you	*Ana jeet gablak*
	Jeet gable minnak
After (time)	*Ba'-ad*
He went after I had seen him.	*Masha' ba'-ad mashufta'h.*
Behind	*Wara' – khalf*
The garden	*Al hadeeka*
The garden is behind you	*Al hadeeka warak*
About	*'an*
I was talking about her.	*Kunt atakalam an-ha'*
Until – till	*Hatta – and*
I want to wait till he comes	*Uridu Antazir hatta ejee*
At	*And-* (or) *Fi*
I was at the hospital	*Kunt and al mustashfa*
Inside – Outside	*Dakhil–barra*
Go inside	*Udkhul Dakhil*
Come outside	*Taal barrá*

N.B.

The prepositions are also used with the accusative pronouns i.e. me, him, her etc., e.g.

From me   *Minni (ana)*   From him   *Minna (huwa)*

The Nominative Pronouns – *ana* – *huwa* etc. are added merely for emphasis.

Far – distant   *Ba'eed.*   Near   *Guareeb* or *Kareeb*

LESSON 24

Formation of Plurals

The plurals are of two types:

(1) Regular (2) irregular. The latter one which must be memorised, is formed by an internal change; e.g.

  pens – pens   *Gualam – Aghlaam* (pl.)
  window(s)   *Nafiza – Nawafiz*
  door(s)   *Ba'-b – be-baan* (pl.)
  donkey(s)   *Hamaar–hameer* (pl.)

(2) The suffix (*in*) is added to the masculine regular noun; e.g.

  Teacher(s)   *Mu-alim – mu-alimin* (pl.)
  Engineer(s)   *Mu'-handez – muhandezeen* (pl.)

(3) Sometimes the noun suffixed with the word (*in*) is an adjective, describing the noun; e.g.

  porter(s)   *Shayal – shayala*
  porter(s)   *Hammal – hammala'*
  porter(s)   *Hammaleen – shayaleen*

but not as a descriptive noun with the word (*in*) The porters of vegetables *Hammalin al khuthara*

(4) For the feminine just add the suffix (*at*) to the regular noun.

(5) Relative Pronouns – who, whom, which, that, are expressed by the word (*illi* or *elli*) for all gender; e.g.

  I saw the man who   (*ana*) *sheft arajel illi kan*
    was with you   *ma'-ak*
  That is the girl who   *Hathik* (*hya*) *al bint illi*
    went with you   *mashet ma'-ak*
  Give me the book   *Atini al kitaab illi huwa*
    which he wants.   *ireeda.*

LESSON 25

Conversation

AT THE CUSTOMS

This is my friend	*Hatha sadeeky*
His name (is) . . .	*Asma sayed . . .*
He (is) an expert in	*Huwa khabeer fi*
petroleum affairs	*shoo-oon al betrool*
He has come from . . .	*Ja', min*
to stay here for . . .	*Hatta yagha-ad hana*
Sometime in . . .	*Ba'ad al wagut fi . . .*
Where (is) the passport . . . ?	*Wein al bassaburt?*
Here *it is* (m.)	*Ahoo* (m.s.) *Ahee* (f.s.)
The visa is from . . .	*At-ta'shira min . . .*
he has . . . suitcases	*And . . . shanaati*
Orders, rules	*Ta'leemaat*
Customs	*Ghumrouk* (or) *Jumruk*
He does not carry anything	*Ma-yah-milish ayeeshey*
For example . . .	*Mathalan*
Tobacco	*Dokhan*
Cigarettes	*Dukhan*
Alcohol	*Kouhool*
Drinks	*Mashroobat*
But	*Leakin*
sure – certainly	*Bitta'-keed*
search – look for	*Fattish*
Anything else	*Shai Akhar*
We thank you	*Nashkurook*
Good bye.	*Ma'assalama*
But to be sure	*La'kin lil ta' keed*
You may search the bags	*Youmkin t'fatish ashanati*

Is there anything else   *Fee ayee-shey akher*
Can we go now?   *Nagh-dar namshoo Al-An*
Certainly   *T'fathaloo* (m.pl.)

EXERCISES BASED ON LESSONS 20 to 25

(1) Translate the following into English:

*Khusoosi Sough Ziyout Raees-al-wazaara Hatha
muwathaf Wein-al-hukuma? Fein-al-jareeda?
Shinu-fi-min-al-akhbaar-al-youm? La-shay-jedeed al-youm.*

(2) Make Arabic questions from these words:

Who? Where? How many? Have you? Is there? What? When?

(3) What time is the following in Arabic?

| 1.5 | 2.10 | 2.15 | 3.20 | 5.25 | 1.20 | 1.25 |
| 1.35 | 1.45 | 4.5 | 8.10 | 7.45 | 9.40 | 6.55 |

(4) Give the opposites of:

*Faqueer Jadeed Taweel Tha-eef Kabeer Kadeem
Rajal Bint Aywa Wesikh Hana Qawi Kam*

(5) Answer these questions:

*Man-anta? Keif-haalak? Man-ma'-ak? Fein masheit
al-youm? Hal-atta'am ala at-tawala? Wein al kalb?*

(6) Translate these into Arabic:

My dear friend.   This is very expensive.   I did not go to my
office today.   When are you going?   I have a report.
No objection.   God forbid!   This is strange.   Nothing.

LESSON 26

Commands or Request

Bring me	*Jeebli*	Give me	*Atini*
Send me	*Arsil-li*	Tell me	*Ghoul-li*
Show me	*Warreni*	Cary this	*Sheel hatha*
Take this away	*Khutu hatha baeed*		
Hurry up	*Isra* or *Bisura*	Wait!	*Arja* or *Estanna*

COMPARATIVES

(1) They are more or less formed on the measure of; e.g.
Bigger   *Ak-bar*   More   *Aktr* (or) *Aktha*

It is formed by the prefix (*a*) and it is connected to the positive adjective and the preposition (*min*) as an antecedent. Also note the change that occurs in the vowel appearing in the positive; i.e. (from i or e to a).
e.g.

Good	*Kuweis – hasan – tayib*
Better	*Akwas – ah'-san – at-yab*
Best	*Al-ah-san*
Big – old	*Kabeer – ak'bar*
Great	*Atheem – A'atham*
More	*Ak-thar*
Bad	*Shein*
Worse	*Ash-yen* or *Arda*
Worst	*Al-arda*

(2) Fore the superlative just add the prefix (*al*) meaning (the) to the comparative; e.g.

The worst book	*Al arda kitaab*
This is the biggest	*Hatha* (*huwa*) *al ak'baar*
This is the best	*Hatha* (*huwa*) *al ah-san*

Vocabulary

Tooth – teeth	*Sin* (s.) *as-naan* (pl.)
My dear friend	*Sadeeghi al aziz*
Dear	*Aziz*
Expensive	*Ghaali*
Most	*Mo'-tham*
Most people	*Mo'-tham-annas*
Also you (m.s.)	*Kathalika enta*
Either . . . or	*Imma . . . wa-imma*
either he or his friend must come here	*Imma huwa wa-imma sadeegha yajib ijee hana*
Neither . . . nor	*La' . . . wa-la'*
neither he nor his friend must come here	*La' huwa wa-la' sadeegha yajib ijee hana*
Must – should – ought	*Yajib* or *laazim*
I did not go to the office today.	*Lam ath-hab ila al-mak-tib al yom.*

N.B.

When using (did not) which is (*lam*) the verb should be in the present tense. e.g.

I did not learn my lesson yesterday	*Lam adres* or *ata-allam Darsi ams*

Please see lesson 19 para (4) dealing with negatives in the present and past tense colloquially while the above examples are in the literary form; i.e. classic.

I must go	*Laazim emshi*
He should go	*Laazim yemshi*
You ought to go	*Laazim temshi*

41

Vocabulary

When are you going to buy a car?	*Amta-treed tshri* (or) *tishri sayaara?*
As soon as I have money.	*Andama ikoon andi filoos*
What are you doing . . . at present (now)	*Matha ta'-mal Fi-al-waght al-haather*
Nothing	*La-shay*
Strange!	*Ghareeb*
What a poor man!	*Mes-keen* (m.) *mes-keena* (f.)
Write a report.	*Iktib tak-reer*
A monthly report	*Tak-reer shah-ri*
May I have my leave!	*Mum-ken akhuth-ijaazati*
when . . . ?	*Amta' . . . !*
Tomorrow, God willing	*Buk-ra in-sha-allah*
For God's sake	*Ar-joock*
Take it next month	*Khuth-ha asha-her attali*
God forbid!	*La-samah-allah.*
That is the end.	*Hathi-hi anna-haya*
Be quiet!	*Es-kit*
Silence	*Si-koot*
What is up?	*Matha-jaraa*
Look here!	*Asma'-* or *esma'*
Look at . . .	*Anthur ila . . .*
I am invited to dinner	*Ana-ma'zoom ala asha*
I have an invitation	*Andi da'waa*
He invited me	*Huma da'-aani*
Have you an invitation card?	*Andak batakat-da'-waa?'*
Of course.	*Tab-an* or *aywa*
Very good	*Kwais*
No objection	*La'-maaneh*

LESSON 27

Verbs

(1) Conjugation of verbs: This differs from other languages. The stem of the verb is the past tense of the third person masculine singular. There is no need of using the Nominative Pronoun with the verb since the prefixes of the present tense and the suffixes of the past tense will indicate to which person they refer.

(2) The future tense is expressed by the present tense. The following table will show the conjugation of the verb:

To drink *Sharaba*   He drank *Sharaba*

N.B. The letter (A) seen at the end of the verb *sharab* (a) in the third person is generally dropped and the verb made short; e.g. He drank. *Sharab*. Conjugatoin of the verb to drink *Sharaba*.

I drank	*Sharubt*	You drank (m.pl.)	*Sharabtu*
You drank (m.s.)	*Sharabt*	You drank (f.pl.)	*Sharabtan*
You drank (f.s.)	*Sharabti*	We drank	*Sharabna*
He drank	*Sharaba*	She drank	*Sharabat*
They drank (m.)	*Sharabu*	They drank (f.)	*Sharaban*

(3) These letters: *'t', 'tu', tan, ti, na, at, u, an.* The indicate the Nominative Pronouns in the past tense.

EXAMPLES

I wrote	*Katab-t*	You wrote	*Latab-tu*
You wrote	*Katab-t*	You wrote	*Katab-tan*
You wrote	*Katab-ti*	We wrote	*Katab-na*
He wrote	*Kataba*	She wrote	*Kataba-t*
They wrote	*Katab-u*	They wrote	*Katab-an*

Verbs

(1) Conjugation of the verb to drink in the present tense:

I drink	*ashrabu*	You drink (m.pl.)	*Tashrabu*
You drink (m.s.)	*Tashrab*	You drink (f.pl.)	*Tashraban*
You drink (f.s.)	*Tashrabi*	She drinks	*Tashrab*
He drinks	*Yashrab*	We drink	*Nashrabu*
They drink (m.)	*Yashrabu*	They drink (f.)	*Yashraban*

(2) Particle of Past Tense: Suffixes.

I	*T*	We	*Na*
You	*T* (m.s.)	He	*A*
You	*Tu* (m.pl.)	She	*At*
You	*Tan* (f.pl.)	They (m.)	*U*
You	*Ti* (f.s.)	They (f.)	*An*

(3) Particles of the Present Tense: Prefixes and Suffixes.

I	*Na*	We	*N...U*
You (m.s.)	*T*	He	*Ya*
You (m.pl.)	*T...U*	She	*T*
You (f.)	*T...I*	They (m.)	*Ya...U*
You (f.)	*T...An*	They (f.)	*Ya...An*

(4) The Imperative of the verb (*Sharaba*) is *Ashrab*. The letter (A) is prefixed to the present tense in most of the verbs.

(5) Verbs 3rd Person (Past Tense) are given first and then their present and the imperative as well.

He heard	*Sama'-a*	He went	*Masha'*
He hears	*Yesma'*	He goes	*Yimshi*
Hear	*Asma*	Go	*Amshi*

(6) The letter (i) is suffixed to the imperative for female: e.g.

Write	*Aktibi*	Take	*Khuti*

LESSON 29

Verbs

He spoke	*Takallama*	He ate	*Akala'*
He speaks	*Yatakallem*	He eats	*Yakel*
speak	*Takallam*	eat	*Kool*
He walked	*Masha'*	He opened	*Fataha*
He walks	*Yimshi*	He opens	*Yafteh*
walk	*Amshi*	open	*Aftah*

N.B.

Now that the rule has been given with regard to the construction of the verbs the infinitive of each verb will be given in English with the three parts in Arabic, to be formed by the student.

To abandon	*Taraka*	*Yat-rak*	*Atrek*
To leave	*Taraka*	*Yat-rak*	*Atrek*
To give up	*Taraka*	*Yat-rak*	*Atrek*
To abhor	*Karaha*	*Yakreh*	*Akrah*
To awake	*Asteikatha*	*Yasteikith*	*Asteikith*
To bind	*Rabata*	*Yarbet*	*Arbet*
To break	*Kassara*	*Yakser*	*Akser*
To choose	*Akhtaar*	*Yakhtaar*	*Akhtaar*
To drive	*Saaga*	*Yasoog*	*Soog*
To forget	*Nasa'*	*Yansa*	*Ansa*
To ride	*Rakiba*	*Yarkib*	*Arkib*
To throw	*Ramaa*	*Yarmi*	*Armi*
To hit	*Tharaba*	*Yathreb*	*Athreb*
To wash	*Ghasala*	*Yaghsel*	*Aghsel*
To write	*Kataba*	*Yakteb*	*Akteb*
To study	*Darasa*	*Yadres*	*Adres*

Verbs

To enter	Dakhala	Yadkhul	Adkhul
To go out	Kharaja	Yakhrej	Akhrej
To play	La-aba	Yal-ab	Al-ab
To laugh	Thahaka	Yath-hek	Ath-hak
To run	Jara	Yaj-ri	Aj-ri
To sit	Jalasa	Yaj-les	Ajles
To see	Shafa	Yashoof	Shoof
To buy	Shara'	Yashri	Ash-ri
To know	Arafa	Ya'-ref	A'-ref
To give	A-ta'	Ya'-ti	A'-ti
To see	Nathara	Yanthir	Anther

N.B. There are two ways by which an Arab sentence is expressed either Nominal or Verbal.

(1) **Nominal**. It starts with a noun, e.g. The man writes his lesson everyday. *Arajel yaktib (fe) darsa kul yom.*

(2) **Verbal**. It starts with a verb. e.g. The man writes his lesson everyday. *Yaktib arajel (fe) darsa kul yom.*

(3) Verbal sentences are frequently used in ordinary speech.

(4) The word (*gha-ad*) is used before verbs to indicate the Present continuous tense. The man is writing his lesson. *Ar-rajel gha-ad yaktib fe darsa.*

N.B. For Past continuous tense the (*kan gha-ad*) is used; e.g.

He was writing his lesson.
Kan gha-ad yaktib (fe) darsa.

but note:

We were writing our lesson.
Kunna gha-adin naktib (fe) darsana.

The word (*gha-adin*) agrees with the pronoun.

Verbs

	3rd Person pa.	pre.	imp.
To kill	{ Katala	Yaktel	Aktel
	or Qatala	Yaqtel	Aqtel
To weep	Baka'	Yabki	Abki
To travel	Saafara	Yesaafer	Saafar
To return	Raja-a	Yer-ja	Ar-ja
To clean	Nathafa	Yenathaf	Nathaf
To wear	Labisa	Yelbis	Albis
To light	Walla-a	Yewalla'	Walla-a
To wish	Raghiba	Yarghib	— —
To wish	Tamanna	Yatamanna	— —
To wish	Wadda	Yawed	— —
To shave	Halaqa	Yaalleq	Ihleq
To marry	Tajawaza	Yatajawiz	Ta'jawiz
To put	Watha-a	Yatha	Thaa'
To swim	Aama	Ya-oom	Oom
To answer	Ajaaba	Youjeeb	Ajib
To sell	Baa-a	Yabeeh	Beeh – beea
To learn	Ta-allama	Yata-allam	Ta-allam
To send	Arsala	Yersell	Arsell
To stand	Wakafa	Yakiff	Kiff or Qif
To arrive	Wasala	Yasell	— —
To dream	Halama	Yah-lim	— —
To rent	Ajjara	You-ajjir	Ajjir
To run	Jaraa	Yaj-ri	Ijri
To enter	Dakhala	Yad-khel	Ad-khel
To play	La-aba	Yal-ab	Al-ab
To repair	Aslaha	Yasaleh	Is-lah
To learn	Darasa	Yad-res	Id-res
To cook	Tabbakha	Yat-bekh	At-Bekh
To receive	Tasallama	Yata-sallem	Tasallem
To resign	Istikaala	Yas-takeel	Is-takeel

VOCABULARY 30

Language	*Loogha*
Weekly	*Us-booee*
Week-end	*Ot-La'h*
May be	*Youmken* or *Ruba'-ma*
Mind you!	*Red-baalak* or *Haaseb!*
Wait a minute	*Dakeeka* or *Lah-tha minfath la*
Mister – Mr.	*Sayed*
Mistress – Mrs.	*Sayeda'*
Mademoiselle	*Aanisa*
Nearby	*Kareeb* or *Qareeb*
Nearly	*Takreeban*
Neighbours	*Jaar* (s.) *Jiraan* (pl.)
What is the news?	*Aish-fi-min-akhbar?*
What is the news?	*Aish-fi-min-jedeed?*
Never mind	*Ma-alesh*
Never	*Aba-dan*
Afterwards	*Ba-dein*
Well-done!	*Ah-sant*
Where are you from?	*Min-aein-enta'?*
What country are you from?	*Min-aein-billad-enta?*
Slowly	*Bish-wash*
Little – small	*Sagheer*
Little (quantity)	*Ka'-leel* or *Qaleel*
By little and little	*shewaya – shewaya*
I speak little Arabic	*Atakalam shewaya araby*
Last Saturday	*Assabt al-maathi*

N.B.

The letter – n – can be used as a prefix for all the verbs in the first person – instead of (*atakalam*) speak – *natakalam*.

VOCABULARY 31

Tax(es)	*Thareeba* (s.) *Tharayeb* (pl.)
Sea	*Bahr*
Seashore	*Shat-el-bahr*
Disease	*Marath* (s.) *Amrath* (pl.)
Clothes	*Malabis*
Trousers	*Sirwal* (s.) *Saraweel* (pl.)
Coat	*Mitaf* (s.) *Maatif* (a.)
Shirt(s)	*Kamis* (s.) *Kumsan* (pl.)
Towel(s)	*Manshif* (s.) *Manaashif* (pl.)
Handkerchief(s)	*Mandeel* (s.) *Manaadeel* (pl.)
Desk	*Mak-taba*
Library(ies)	*Mak-taba* (s.) *Mak-tabaat* (pl.)
Offices(s)	*Mak-tab* (s.) *Makaatib* (pl.)
Servant (m.s.)	*Khaddam*
Servant (f.s.)	*Khaddama*
Sweeper	*Kannas*
Car(s)	*Saeeyara* (s.) *Saeeyaraat* (pl.)
Town(s)	*Madeena* (s.) *Muden* (pl.)
Street(s)	*Shara'* (s.) *Shewaara'* (pl.)
Watch(es)	*Sa'-a'* (s.) *Sa'-aat* (pl.)
Clock(s)	*Sa-a'* (s.) *Sa-aat* (pl.)
Hotel	*Hoteil* or *Funduk*
Driver(s)	*Sawaagh* (s.) *Sawagueen* (pl.)
Edifice	*Eemaara* or *Bi-naaya*
Princedom	*Eemaara*
Shop(s)	*Dukkaan-Da'-Kakeen* (pl.)
Trip	*Rih-la'h* or *Fus-ha'*
Airport	*Ma'-taar*
Cairo Airport	*Ma'-taar-Al-Cahira*
Aswan Airport	*Ma'-taar-Aswan*

EXERCISES BASED ON LESSONS 26 TO 31

(1) Give the Past Tense of these verbs:

*Yatrak   Yakreh   Yasteikith   Yarkib   Yaghsel
Yadress   Yatajawiz   Ya-oom   Yatakallem
You-ajjir.*

(2) Conjugate these verbs into Present Tense:
Nasa (use the prefixes and the suffixes) *Aktaar
Rabata   Rakiba   Tharaba   Ramaa   Dakhala
Kharaja   La-aba-Thahanka   Jara   Jalasa.*

(3) Memorise the verbs.

(4) Translate the following into Arabic:

He may come tomorrow. Mr. Ali is out of the office.
I want to see you afterwards. No, I never come here.
(*la-man-jeesh abadan hana*) My neighbours (are) not
here. They (are) outside. I speak little Arabic but I
learn your language. Whose is this mademoiselle?
Where are you from? Come here slowly. What time
is it? Where are we? Nobody knows what time it is.
Where is your passport? What is the trouble? why
(are) you crying? In your letter (of) last Saturday you
asked me (to) give you some information about my
country. What (is) the name (of) this street? My
driver (has) not come today. Whose edifice (is) this?
I must go now to the market. Come with me. I am
going to the airport. My clothes. That is your library.
I (am) not responsible. It is his responsibilty.
Something reasonable.

VOCABULARY 32

Responsible	*Mass-ool*
Responsibilty	*Mass-oolya*
Population	*Sukkaan*
Witness(es)	*Shaahid* (s.) *Shuhood* (pl.)
Debt(s)	*Dayn* (s.) *Deyoun* (pl.)
Reasonable	*Maa-guool*
Policy	*Seayasa*
Politics	*Ash-shu-oon aseayasiya*
The Press	*Asahaafa*
King	*Malik*
Kings	*Mulook*
Queen(s)	*Malika* (s.) *Malikaat* (pl.)
Prince(s)	*Amir* (m.) *Amira* (f.)
Wife	*Zouja*
Husband	*Zouj*
Anyone	*Ayeewahed*
Everyone	*Kull-wahed*
Cup of coffee	*Finjan ghah-wa*
Cup of tea	*Kas shehi*
Cup of water	*Kas moya*
Myself	*Nafsi*
Yourself	*Naf-sak* (m.s.)
Himself	*Naf-sa'h*
Herself	*Naf-saha*
Ourselves	*Naf-sana*
Yourselves	*Naf-sakum* (m.pl.)
Yourselves	*Naf-saken* (f.pl.)

VOCABULARY 33

Body	*Jessm* or *Jessem*
Head(s)	*Raas* (s.) *Ru-oos* (pl.)
Face	*Wa'-jh* (or) *Wa'-jih*
Eye(s)	*Ayn* (s.) *Ayoun* (pl.)
Ear(s)	*Withn* (s.) *With-nei* (pl.)
Nose	*Anef*
Mouth	*Fam*
Tooth (teeth)	*Sinn* (s.) *As-naan* (pl.)
Tongue	*Lisaan*
Hair	*Sha'-arr*
Hand(s)	*Yad* (s.) *Yedein* (pl.)
Foot (feet)	*Rejel* (s.) *Arjul* (pl.)
Blood	*Damm*
The breakfast	*Al-fetoor*
The lunch	*Al-ghada'*
The dinner	*Al-asha'*
Salt	*Melh* (or) *Melah*
Pepper	*Filfill*
Oil	*Zeit* (s.) *Zi-yout* (pl.)
Bread	*Khub-za*
Egg(s)	*Beitha* (s.) *Beith* (pl.)
Knife(ves)	*Moos.* (s.) *Amwas* (pl.)
Beer	*Birra*
Wine	*Nbeet*
Mineral Water	*Moya-ma-daniya*
Lemon	*Lay-moon* (or) *Leem*
Orange	*Bur-t-guaal*
Apples	*Teffah* (pl.) *Tefaha* (s.)
Banana(s)	*Mouza* (s.) *Mouz* (pl.)
Salad	*Salaata*
Lettuce	*Khass*

VOCABULARY 34

The Post Office	*Al-bareed*
The Cable	*Al-telegraf*
The Bank	*Al-masraf*
The Cheque	*Ash-sheik*
One Dinar	*Wa'had Dinaar*
Two Dinars	*Dinarein*
Three Dinars	*Talaata Dinaraat*
½ Dinar	*Nefs Dinaar*
¼ Dinar	*Ruba Dinaar*
One Dirham	*Dirham*
Five Dirhams	*Khamsa Darahum*
Ten Dirhams	*Ashratu Darahim*
100 Dirhams	*Miyat Dirham*
1000 Dirhams	*Alf Dirham*
Once	*Marra'-waheda*
Twice	*Marratein*
Three times	*Thalaata-marraat*
Four times	*Arba'-marraat*
Last year	*Assana'-al maathya*
Heat	*Harr*
Hot	*Saakhin* (or) *Haamy*
Cold	*Baared* (or) *Bard*
Warm	*Daafy*
Rain	*Matar* (s.) *Amtaar* (pl.)
Mountain(s)	*Jebel* (s.) *Ajbaal* (pl.)
Traffic	*Muroor*
Jam	*Izdiham*, (*Zahma*) colloq.

VOCABULARY 35

Budget	*Mizaneeya*
Expenditure	*Mas-roofaat*
Revenue	*Eeradat*
Council	*Maj-lis*
Government(s)	*Hukooma* (s.)
	Hukoomat (pl.)
Foreign Ministry	*Wazaarat al-Khaarijiya*
Armed Forces	*Al-Qoowaat al-Musallaha*
Civil Service	*Al-Khidma al-Madaniya*
Revolutionary Command Council	*Majis Qeeyaadat Athawra*
Ministry of Interior	*Wazaarat Addakhilya*
Ministry of Communication	*Wazaarat Al Muasallat*
Ministry of Defence	*Wazaarat Al Defaa'*
Ministry of Education	*Wazaarat At-ta'-leem*
Ministry of Information	*Wazaarat Al-i-laam*
Ministry of Health	*Wazaarat As-Sehha*
Ministry of Labour	*Wazaarat Al-amal*
Ministry of Economy	*Wazaarat Al-i-ktisaad*
Ministry of Industry	*Wazaarat As-Sinaa-a'*
Ministry of Agriculture	*Wazaarat Az-Zirraa'-a'*
Ministry of Petrol	*Wazaarat Annaft*
Ministry of Finance	*Wazaarat Al-Kizana*
Ministry of Justice	*Wazaarat Al-Adl*
Ministry of State	*Wazaarat Ad-Dowla'*
Ministry of Housing	*Wazaarat Al-Iskaan*
The Egyptian Government	*Al-Hukooma Al. Masria*

VOCABULARY 36

Right	*Yameen*
On your right	*Ala-yameenak* (m.)
Left	*Shemaal*
On your left	*Ala-shemaalak* (m.)
East(erly)	*Shargh – sharqy*
West(erly)	*Gharb-b – gharby*
Western	*Ghar-by*
South	*Jenoob*
North	*Shamaal*
Season(s)	*Fasl* (s.) *Fusool* (pl.)
Winter	*Sheta'*
Autumn	*Khareef*
Spring	*Rabee'*
Summer	*Say-if*
Colour(s)	*Loan* (s.) *Alwaan* (pl.)
White	*Ab-yath*
Red	*Ahh-marr*
Black	*Aswad*
Yellow	*As-far*
Green	*Akh-Thar*
Tomato	*Temaatam*
Banana	*Mouz*
Onion	*Ba'-sal*
Carrots	*Jazar*
Dates	*Tamar*
Cucumber	*Khiyar*
Parsley	*Ma-danoos*

VOCABULARY 37

Formal official	*Rasmi*
Crime(s)	*Jareema* (s.) *Jaraa-im* (pl.)
Criminal(s)	*Muj-rem* (s.)
	Muj-rimeen (pl.)
Offence (Traffic)	*Mukhalafa*
Scene(s)	*Manthar* (s.) *Manaather* (pl.)
Request(s)	*Talab* (s.) *Talabaat* (pl.)
I have no spare time	*Ma-endish wagut faragh*
Farewell	*Widaa-an* (or) *Ma'-assalama*
Kerosine	*Ghaz*
Out of order	*Mu-attal – Khasran*
Spare parts	*Kitaa-ghiyaar*
Always	*Day-man*
Constantly	*Day-man*
Rare	*Naa-dir*
Rarely	*Naa-dir*
Relative(s)	*Kareeb* (s.) *Akaarib* (pl.)
A Nurse	*Mumarritha* (f.)
Belt	*Hezaam*
Parliament	*Barlamaan*
Politics	*Al-umoor-asseyasya*
Ministry	*Wazaara*
Department	*Mas-laha* (or) *Idaara*
Section(s)	*Qissim* (s.) *Aq-saam* (pl.)
Decision	*Karaar* (or) *Qaraar*
Council (meeting)	*Ej-timaa'*
Urgent	*Musta'-jel*
Signature	*Taw-keeh*
Signature	*Im-thaa*

Vocabulary

Beautiful	*Jameel*
Family	*A-eela'* (or) *Ay-la*
My family	*A-eelati* (or) *Ayl-ti*
Your family	*A-eelatak* (see lesson 3) (suffixes)
Wise	*Aaqel*
Clever	*Thakey* (or) *Dakey*
Stupid	*Ghabee*
Ignorant	*Jaahel*
Courageous	*Shoojaa*
Coward	*Jabaan*
Generous	*Kareem*
Success	*Najaah*
Question	*Soo-aal*
Answer	*Jawaab*
Absent	*Ghaa-ib*
Present	*Moujud* (or) *Moujood*
Serious	*Khateer*
Crises	*Az-ma'*
Crisis	*Azamaat*
Demonstration	*Muthaahara*
Problem	*Mush-kela*
Secret	*Sir* (s.) *As-raar* (pl.)
Fear	*Khouf*
Fearful	*Mukheef*
Protest	*Ih-teejaaj*
Insurance	*Ta'-meen*
Resignation	*Istikaala*
Independence	*Istik-laal*
Independent	*Mustakill*

LESSON 39

Vocabulary

Farm – Farmer	*Maz-ra' – Muzaareh*
Animal(s)	*Hay-waan* (s.) *– Hay-wanaat* (pl.)
Plant(s)	*Shajara* (s.) *Ash-jaar* (pl.)
Dog(s)	*Kalb* (s.) *Keylaab* (pl.)
Kitchen	*Mat-bakh*
Refrigerator	*Tallaja*
Electricity	*Kah-raba*
Gaz	*Ghaaz*
Bedroom	*Hujrat-annoum*
Dining room	*Hujrat-al-akel*
Sitting room	*Hujrat-al-jeloos*
Bathroom	*Hammam*
Dish(es)	*Sahn* (s.) *Suhun* (pl.)
Spoon(s)	*Miil aka Maalik*
Fork(s)	*Shoka* (s.) *Shewak* (pl.)
Carpet	*Sajada* (or) *Bisaat*
Oven(s)	*Furn* (s.) *Afraan* (pl.)
Stove(s)	*Daffaya* (s.) *Daffayaat* (pl.)
Bell(s)	*Jaras* (s.) *Aj-raas* (pl.)
Soap	*Saboon*
Seat(s)	*Mak-ad* (s.) *Makaa-ad* (pl.)
Conference(s)	*Mu'-tamar'* (s.) *Mu'-tamaraat* (pl.)
Port-harbour(s)	*Mina'* (s.) *Mawaani* (pl.)
Watchman	*Haaris* (or) *Ghafeer*
Fire(s)	*Naar* (s.) *Niraan* (pl.)
Theft	*Sirgha*
Thief	*Saaregh* or *Saraagh* or *Luss*
Cupboard(s)	*Dulaab* (or) *Duwaleeb* (pl.)
Picture(s)	*Soora* (s.) *Suwar* (pl.)
Age	*Umr*
Still	*Mazaal*

LESSON 40

Vocabulary

Birth	*Wilaada*
Death	*Mout*
Barber	*Hallaq*
The Royal Palace	*Addiwan-al-malekye*
H. R. H. Palace	*Diwan-samoo-al-amir*
Royal Decree	*Marsoom-malekey*
Head of the Royal Palace	*Rais-addiwaan-al-malekye*
Individual(s)	*Fard* (s.) *Af-raad* (pl.)
Commerce	*Tijaara*
Trader(s)	*Taajer* (s.) *Tujaar* (pl.)
Gain – profit	*Ribah* (s.) *Arbaah* (pl.)
Suit(s)	*Bad-la* (s.) *Bidel* (pl.)
Ring(s)	*Khaatim* (s.)
	Khawaatim (pl.)
Gold	*Thahab*
Silver	*Fiddah*
Agreement	*Itifaaq*
Simple	*Baseet* (or) *Sahell*
Difficult	*Sa-ab*
Love	*Hoobb*
Progress	*Takadum*
Money	*Filoos* (or) *Nukood*
Chicken	*Dajaaja*
Chief	*Rais* (or) *Za-eem*
Dry	*Naashef* (or) *Yaabis*
It differs from	*Yakhtalif min . . .*
In effect	*Fi-al-wakah* (or) *Hakikatan*
To no effect	*Mafish-faa-ida*
How old are you?	*Kam um-rak?* (m.)
What tribe are you from?	*Min-ain kabila enta?*

59

EXERCISES BASED ON LESSONS 32 TO 40

(1) Give the opposites of:

   *Kwais   Kabeer   Bard   Hanaak   Qareeb
   Jameel   Jabaan   Jawaab   Ghaa-ib   Ghabee
   Wilaada*

(2) Answer these questions:

   *Mann hath-ratak?   Kam um-rak?   Min ain qabila
   enta?   Fein saaken?   Fi-ain-sharika tesh-tigul?
   Hatha-shai-naadir.   Maza-al-yom fi ajjareeda?
   Hathi sharika mus-takilla.*

(3) Translate the following into Arabic:

   I want to wait here till he comes. Come outside. The
   food is on the table. How is your family? How much
   money have you? I am going to the barber. Is there
   any problem. My servant (did) not come today. Call
   the sweeper, please. I (did) not take any decision.
   The oven is still hot. What is the colour of your car?

(4) Use each of these words in a sentence:

   *Abadan   Ba-dein   Yameen   Day-man   Jameel
   Musta-jel   Ghaa-ib   Mu-attal   Sa-ab   Bad-la
   Hamman   Thakey   Mu-tamar   Naar*

Vocabulary

God	*Allah*
Heaven	*Allah*
Bible	*Attaw-raat*
Coran	*Al-qur-an* or *Koran*
Jew	*Yahoodi* (s.) *Yahood* (pl.)
Gospel	*Al-an-jeel*
Christian	*Maseehi* (s.) *Maseehien* (pl.)
Church	*Kaneesa* (s.) *Kana-iss* (pl.)
Bishop	*Osqoff*
Priest-Monk	*Raahib* or *Qissis'*
Nun	*Raahiba* or *Qassisa*
Clergyman	*Qassis* or *Raahib*
Convent	*Dayer* or *Kineesa*
Christmas	*Id-al-milaad*
Easter	*Id-al-fasah*
Posque	*Id-al-fasah*
Moslem	*Muslim* (s.) *Muslimeen* (pl.)
Pilgrim	*Haj* (s.) *Hajjaj* (pl.)
Quarter	*Ru-ba'*
Third	*Thilth*
Half	*Nassif*
Mosque	*Jamaa* (s.) *Jawaa-ma* (pl.)
Minaret	*Ma'-thana* or *Manara*
Preacher	*Wa-ath* or *Wa-ed* (or) *Imaan*
Believer	*Moo-men* (s.) *Moo-meneen* (pl.)

Infidel	*Kaafer* (s.) *Kuffaar* (pl.)
Atheist	*Kaafer* (s.) *Kuffaar* (pl.)
Paradise	*Jenna*
Hell	*Ja-hannem*
Fanatic	*Muta-assab* (s.) *Muta-assibeen* (pl.)
Apostle	*Rasool* (s.) *Rus-sul* (pl.)
Angel	*Malaak* (s.) *Malaa-ika* (pl.)
Devil	*Shai-taan* (s.) *Shay-ateen* (pl.)
Election	*In-tikhabaat*
Vote	*Soat* (s.) *As-waat* (pl.)
Ambassador	*Safeer* (s.) *Sufara'* (pl.)
Embassy	*Safaara* (s.) (pl.)
Declaration	*Tas-reeh*
Consul	*Qun-sel*
Consulate	*Qunsoolia*
Delegation	*Wafd* (s.) *Woofood* (pl.)
Municipality	*Baladia* (s.) *Baladiyaat* (pl.)

N.B.

Plurals are inserted where necessary.

Tailor	*Tar-zi*
Blacksmith	*Hadaad* (s.) *Haddadeen* (pl.)
Baker	*Khabaaz* (s.) *Khabbazeen* (pl.
Fishmonger	*Baaya-samak* (s.) *Sammakin* (pl.)
Butcher	*Jazzaar* (s.) *Jazzareen* (pl.)
Grocer	*Baqaal* (s.) *Baqaleen* (pl.)
Green-Grocer	*Khadar* (s.) *Khadareen* (pl.)
Teacher'	*Mudariss* (s.) *Mudarrisin* (pl.

Carpenter	*Najar* (s.) *Najareen* (pl.)
Painter	*Nakkash* (s.) *Nakkashin* (pl.)
Cook	*Tabaakh* (s.) *Tabaakheen* (pl.)
Waiter	*Saf-raji* (s.) *Saf-rajiah* (pl.)
Farmer	*Muzaareh* (or) *Fellah* (s.) *Fellaheen* (pl.)
Peasant	*Muzaareh* (or) *Fellah* (s.) *Fellaheen* (pl.)
Broker	*Samsar* (s.) *Samsara* (pl.)
Sweeper	*Kannas* (s.) *Kannaseen* (pl.)
Doorkeeper	*Bawaab* (s.) *Bawaabeen* (pl.)
Cab-man	*Arabaaji* (s.) *Arabajiah* (pl.)
Thief	*Liss* (s.) *Lussus* (pl.)
Midwife	*Qaabila* (s.) *Qablat* (pl.)
Translator	*Mutarjim*
Watch maker	*Saa-aati* (s.)
Messenger	*Muraasil* or *Mubashir*
Dentist	*Tabeeb asnaan*
Oculist	*Tabeeb ayoun*
Photographer	*Musawaraati* or *Musawar*
Hammer	*Mat-ragha*
Nail	*Mesmaar* (s.) *Masameer* (pl.)
Scissors	*Maqass*
Vessel	*Eena*
Lid or cover	*Ghataa*
Pot	*Ghedre* (s.) *Ghedoor* (pl.)
Pan	*Tanjara* (s.) *Tanjair* (pl.)
Rope	*Habl*
Grandfather	*Jad* (s.) *Judood* (pl.)

Grandmother	*Jadda* (s.) *Jaddat* (pl.)
Nephew (m. & f.)	*Ibn akh* (m.)
	Ibn ukht (f.)
Niece	*Bent ukht*
	Bent akh
Uncle	*Am* or *Khaal*
Aunt	*Amma* or *Khaala*
Widower	*Armal*
Widow	*Armala*
Bride	*Aroos* or *Aroosa* (s.) *Ara-es* (pl.)
Bridegroom	*Arees* (s.) *Erssan* (pl.)
Honeymoon	*Shahar al asal*
Surname	*Laqeb* (s.) *Alqab* (pl.)
Melons	*Shammam*
Watermelon	*Beteekh*
Raisins	*Zibeeb*
Figs	*Teen*
Once more	*Marra ukhra* or *Tani*
Put out	*At-fee* or *Ta'fee*
Right away	*Halan*
Switch off	*At-fee* or *Ta'fee*
Switch on	*Ash-al*
Sooner or later	*Aa-jilan am 'aj-lan*
How old are you?	*Kam omrak*
Generosity	*Karam*
Misery	*Bukhul*
Ashamed	*Khajul* or *Met'hasheem*
Rude	*Qalil al adap*